The DMZ

KOREA ESSENTIALS No. 3

The DMZ: Dividing the Two Koreas

First Published in 2010 by Seoul Selection
B1 Korean Publishers Association Bldg., 105-2 Sagan-dong,
Jongno-gu, Seoul 110-190, Korea
Phone: (82-2) 734-9567
Fax: (82-2) 734-9562
Email: publisher@seoulselection.com
Website: www.seoulselection.com

ISBN: 978-89-91913-75-2   04080
ISBN: 978-89-91913-70-7   (set)
Printed in the Republic of Korea

The DMZ

Dividing the Two Koreas

Korea Foundation
한국국제교류재단

Seoul Selection

CONTENTS

Appendix
Tours of the DMZ 98
More about the Korean War 99

Delving Deeper

INTRODUCTION

Four kilometers wide and stretching 250 km from the East Sea to the West Sea, the Korean Demilitarized Zone divides the Korean Peninsula roughly in half, with the Republic of Korea to the south and the Democratic People's Republic of Korea to the north. Born of the fratricidal Korean War, it is perhaps the oldest continuous symbol of the Cold War and a tense border separating the two halves of the world's last divided nation, where democracy and communism still glare at one another in mutual animosity. Nowhere is this more evident than at the Joint Security Area (JSA) near the so-called "truce village" of Panmunjeom, where South Korean and North Korean soldiers stand practically face to face, the hostility almost palpable.

The DMZ is more than just a hostile frontier, though. The DMZ's status as a virtual no-man's-land has resulted in the four kilometer wide belt transforming into a spectacular nature preserve, home to countless rare plants and animals. Its scenic beauty has led to calls for its preservation as a park even after Korean reunification. Biologists are careful to note, however, that contrary to popular claims, the environment in the DMZ is far from pristine—it is the product of a multitude of human stresses on the local ecology, and efforts are urgently needed to protect and recover this unique environmental legacy of the Cold War.

This book introduces the Korean DMZ and its impact on Korean history, culture and ecology. Chapter One, "The Last Cold War Frontier," defines the DMZ and examines its many unique features. Chapter Two, "The Korean War," introduces that tragic conflict, a knowledge of which is essential to understanding the DMZ. Chapter Three looks at Panmunjeom and the JSA, the heart of the DMZ and a poignant Cold War icon. Chapter Four, "Home to Nature Evolving," surveys the fragile natural environment of the DMZ and refutes common misconceptions regarding its ecological condition. Chapter Five, "The DMZ as a Museum," introduces the many historical and cultural relics located in and around the DMZ.

"The scariest place on Earth"

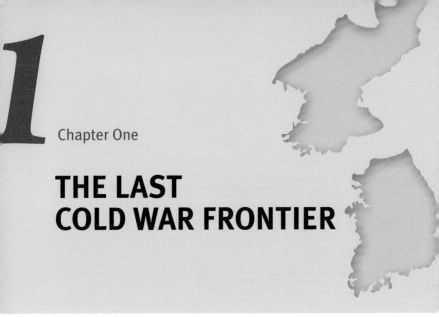

Chapter One

THE LAST
COLD WAR FRONTIER

The fall of the Berlin Wall might have signified the end of the Cold War in much of the rest of the world, but in East Asia the Korean Demilitarized Zone—better known by its acronym, DMZ—remains as the last Cold War frontier. About four kilometers wide and 250 kilometers long, the DMZ cuts the Korean Peninsula roughly in half, running from the mouth of the Hangang River in the west to the coastal village of Myeongho-ri in the east, crossing at an angle the 38th Parallel (see p16). To the north lies the Democratic People's Republic of Korea, or North Korea, one of the world's last remaining outposts of communism and a society largely closed to the outside world. To the south lies the Republic of Korea, or South Korea, a vibrant democracy and global economic power that has become one of the world's largest trading states.

Despite what the name might imply, the DMZ is far from demilitarized. It is, in fact, one of the most militarized frontiers on the planet, bristling with watchtowers, razor wire, land mines, tank traps, and heavy weaponry. Visiting the DMZ in 1993, former US President Bill Clinton called it "the scariest place on Earth." Nowhere in the world are international tensions more palpable than at the Joint Security Area (JSA) near the so-called "truce village" of Panmunjeom.

The DMZ might mark the starkest political border in the world, with the Cold War contrast between communism and democracy thrown into sharp relief. The economic contrast is even more dramatic, as is best illustrated by a now famous photograph, taken from space, of the Korean Peninsula at night: below the DMZ is a nation awash in lights, while above the DMZ there is almost nothing but darkness. The divide is made all the more impressive by the fact that North and South Koreans share a common language, a common culture, and a (largely) common historical heritage, against which the last 65 years is only a blip.

North Korean soldiers in steel helmets and South Korean and US soldiers stare at one another across the Military Demarcation Line.

BIRTH OF THE DMZ

The DMZ was born on July 27, 1953, when the Chinese, North Koreans, and UN Command signed the Korean Armistice Agreement, bringing a ceasefire to the Korean War. From the front line, the Chinese and North Koreans pulled their forces back 2 km north, while the UN Command pulled its forces back 2 km south, creating in the middle a four kilometer no-man's-land. This four-kilometer strip of land runs 250 km from the east coast of the peninsula to the west, crossing the 38th Parallel at an angle, and has served as the dividing line between North and South Korea to the present day.

When most people think of the DMZ, they think of imposing barbed wire fences manned by soldiers in guard posts. These do exist at the DMZ, but at the Northern and Southern Limit Lines, marking the boundaries of the Demilitarized Zone. As a matter of fact, the DMZ is composed of several different parts. Running through the middle of the DMZ is the Military Demarcation Line

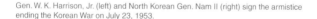

Gen. W. K. Harrison, Jr. (left) and North Korean Gen. Nam Il (right) sign the armistice ending the Korean War on July 23, 1953.

Rusting signs marking the MDL

(MDL), the true border between North and South Korea. It is marked by nothing more than a string of small, rusting, yellow metal signs, placed at 200 m intervals along the its length. Reflecting the makeup of the combatants of the Korean War, the signs are written in English and Korean on one side and Chinese and Korean on the other. The UN is responsible for maintaining 696 of the signs, while the communists are responsible for maintaining the other 696.

To the north of the MDL is a two kilometer buffer zone, matched by a two kilometer buffer zone to the south. North Korean troops patrol the northern buffer zone, while South Korean and, until recently, UN (almost entirely American) troops patrol the southern buffer zone. In accordance with the Armistice, however, large troop concentrations and heavy weapons like tanks and artillery are forbidden in the DMZ, as are the basing of troops and the construction of military

North Korea

Pyongyang

MDL

Panmunjeom

NLL
SLL   Seoul

■ DMZ: Demilitarized Zone
--- MDL: Military Demarcation Line

South Korea

Scenery near the DMZ at Cheorwon. The DMZ is distinguished by thick greenery. In front of it are the golden fields of South Korea's Cheorwon Plain. On the other side is North Korea's Pyeonggang Plateau.

facilities. The northern and southern limits of the DMZ, designated the Northern Limit Line and Southern Limit Line, are marked by a series of barbed wire fences.

According to the 1953 Armistice, neither side is allowed to cross the MDL. There was an exception to this: in the Joint Security Area, a "truce village" where negotiations between the Korean War combatants took place, personnel from both sides used to be able to roam freely. Following the killing of two US Army officers in an incident in 1976 (see p22), however, movement has been restricted to the respective sides of the MDL in the JSA, too, with the lone exception of the Military Armistice Commission Conference Room, a small building bisected by the MDL. Within this room, people are free to step across the MDL.

An agreement signed soon after the Armistice barred civilians from living in the DMZ, save for two villages, one on the southern side of the MDL and one on the northern side (see p18). On the MDL itself, there is also the so-called "truce village" of

South Korean MP stands guard in the Military Armistice Commission Conference Room, the only place where people are free to step across the MDL.

Panmunjeom; the original village has largely disappeared, save for the building where the Korean Armistice Agreement was signed, which is now a North Korean museum. In South Korea, there is another line in addition to the DMZ, coined the "Civilian Control Line," which extends 5 to 20 km from the southern edge of the DMZ. Designated by the 8th US Army Command in February 1954, the unmarked line was established to protect military

THE 38TH PARALLEL

In common, everyday Korean parlance, "the 38th Parallel" (Sampal-seon) is frequently used as a synonym for the DMZ. In fact, however, the two are very different things.

The 38th Parallel was the line where the Korean Peninsula was first divided into two occupational zones in 1945. Interestingly, the line was recommended by two US Army colonels—Dean Rusk and Charles Bonesteel—using a *National Geographic* map in the middle of the night. The decision took only 30 minutes, but it would have a lasting impact. South of the 38th Parallel, the Americans set up an occupational regime that would later become the Republic of Korea, or South Korea. North of the 38th Parallel, the Soviets set up an occupational regime of their own, which would later become North Korea.

The Korean War (see Chapter 2), however, made the 38th Parallel irrelevant as North Korean forces crossed the parallel to invade the South. The irrelevance of the line was further cemented when UN

UN forces retreat across the 38th Parallel, the pre-war boundary between North and South Korea, in 1950.

facilities near the DMZ. Movement of civilians in and out of this zone is strictly controlled, although the roughly 19,000 people of the 51 villages located north of the line may come and go as they like. Nearby farmers may tend land in the area, too, if they follow the proper procedures. The territory of 14 cities and counties in two provinces and one metropolitan city lies inside this zone.

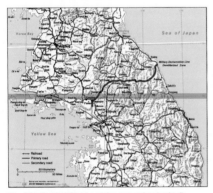

The 38th Parallel (blue) and the current border (red).

forces, then on the counterattack, crossed the line in a bid to unite the peninsula under the South. As the war ground to a stalemate, however, the military front line eventually settled near the 38th Parallel, in fact crossing it at an angle. After three years of war, North and South finished pretty much where they had started, at least territorially.

That said, today's DMZ does not follow the 38th Parallel exactly. In the west, near Seoul, the DMZ is largely south of the 38th Parallel, leaving cities such as Gaeseong—formerly South Korean—under Northern rule. In the central region, however, the line swings northward above the 38th Parallel and for the most part continues at a northward angle until it reaches the East Sea coast, placing many formerly North Korean-run towns under South Korean administration. Evidence of this can found in the South Korean town of Cheorwon, where the ruins of the old local headquarters of the Workers' Party of Korea—the ruling party of North Korea—stand to this day (see p82).

A Tale of Two Villages

The 1953 Armistice allowed for the creation of two civilian villages in the DMZ, one South Korean and one North Korean. These villages, located near Panmunjeom, are Daeseong-dong (Freedom Village) in the South and Gijeong-dong (Propaganda Village) in the North.

PROPAGANDA VILLAGE

Just 800 m from the Military Demarcation Line in North Korea is the village of Gijeong-dong. Known in the South as "Propaganda Village" (the North prefers the term "Peace Village"), the village is officially home to a 200-family collective farm. Observers, however, believe the village to be empty and most of its buildings to be merely concrete shells without windows or rooms. It is, however, home to the world's tallest flagpole, a 160 m tower from which hangs a massive 270 kg flag (the flag is taken down in the rain, as the extra weight would rip the flag from the tower). The super-tall flagpole was the result of a brief "flagpole war" in the 1980s with nearby Daeseong-dong, home to an impressively sized 100 meter flagpole.

JSA

NORTHERN LIMIT LINE

JSA (Joint Security Area)

MDL

Propaganda Village

Freedom Village

SOUTHERN LIMIT LINE

Military Demarcation Line

FREEDOM VILLAGE

Daeseong-dong—administratively speaking, the village of Josan-ri in Gunnae-myeon, Paju City—was founded by villagers who lived in the area prior to the war. Just 0.6 km from Panmunjeom, it is home to about 200 people, mostly farmers. Unlike other Korean villages, it is under the control not of the Republic of Korea, but rather of the United Nations Command, which is responsible for its defense. Despite this, residents are regarded as South Korean citizens, with the right to vote and receive an education.

Life in the village is subject to a number of restrictions. Outsiders may not move to the village. To maintain their residency rights, villagers must spend at least 240 days in the village. They are subject to an 11 pm curfew, enforced by the UN Command. Still, it has its perks as well: technically speaking, residents cannot own property (instead, they are given lifetime leases), so they are free from paying property taxes. Their sons are also exempt from military service. The government also provides villagers with a number of additional benefits and subsidies.

US soldiers interacting with children in the DMZ as part of the USFK Good Neighbor program.

DEMILITARIZED OR MILITARIZED?

While the term "demilitarized zone" might suggest otherwise, the area around the DMZ—and indeed, the DMZ itself—is extremely militarized. As a peace treaty has yet to be signed (indeed, South Korea, which objected to the peace talks, is not even a party to the Armistice), both sides remain technically at war. The bulk of the North Korean and South Korean armies—both among the world's largest—are deployed within a short distance of the zone. The United States, too, maintains a sizable military presence at Dongducheon, a city not far from the line. The countryside bristles with military facilities of all sorts. Within the DMZ itself, both sides man guard posts and conduct regular patrols.

Perhaps unsurprisingly, the DMZ has witnessed many clashes and

skirmishes since the signing of the Armistice. The worst period of violence was between 1966 and 1969, when North Korea used deepening American involvement in Vietnam to test US commitments to South Korea. In that three-year period, 299 South Korean soldiers and 43 US soldiers were killed in a wave of North Korean provocations at the DMZ (see p22). The DMZ is also filled with mine fields.

South Korean soldiers patrol the iron fence of the Southern Limit Line, the southern boundary of the DMZ.

MILITARY FORCE COMPARISON IN 2008   (Source: Global Fire Power)

South Korea		North Korea
48,379,392	Population	23,479,088
26,721,668	Military Manpower	12,414,017
687,000	Active Military Personnel	1,170,000
4,500,000	Active Military Reserves	4,700,000
538	Air-Based Weapons	1,778
8,325	Land-Based Weapons	16,400
85	Naval Units	708
$25.5 billion	Defense Budget / Expenditure	$5.5 billion
$262.2 billion	Foreign Reserves	$0

While the DMZ has been the scene of more than its fair share of bloodshed, it has also had its moments of hope. In 1992, the two Koreas agreed to reconnect railroad links severed in the Korean War. On September 18, 2002, groundbreaking ceremonies to reconnect the western Seoul—Shinuiju Line and eastern East Sea Line were held. Inter-Korean highways through the DMZ were completed in 2004. On May 17, 2007, trains traveled through the DMZ for the first time since 1950, followed soon after by daily freight service. On October 2, 2007, then South Korean President Roh Moo-hyun crossed the Military Demarcation Line on foot to attend the second inter-Korean summit.

Train pulls in at Imjingang Station. (left) Trucks full of South Korean aid cross the DMZ into North Korea. (middle) Late South Korean President Roh Moo-hyun walks across the MDL. (right)

INCIDENTS AT THE DMZ

Since the conclusion of the Korean War, the DMZ has been the site of many incidents, both large and small. Major events include:

DMZ CONFLICT OF 1966-1969

While the Vietnam War raged in Southeast Asia, the North Koreans moved to test US security commitments to South Korea by initiating a series of provocations along the DMZ. Beginning in 1966 and petering out in 1969, this period would prove the bloodiest in the history of the DMZ. In the worst year, 1968, there were 181 serious violations in and around the DMZ, resulting in the deaths of 145 South Korean and 17 US soldiers. Things got so bad along the DMZ that the US Department of Defense declared the area a hostile fire zone, allowing US soldiers serving in the area to collect additional pay.

The conflict along the DMZ was highlighted by the January 21, 1968, raid on the South Korean presidential mansion by 31 North Korean commandos in a bid to assassinate President Park Chung-hee. Disguised as South Korean soldiers, the commandos got within 800 m of the presidential mansion before they were recognized and stopped in a firefight. The commandos attempted to flee back to North Korea, but a South Korean-US manhunt killed 29 of them. One was captured, and another committed suicide.

THE AXE MURDER INCIDENT AND OPERATION PAUL BUNYAN

One of the more notorious incidents along the DMZ took place in the Joint Security Area (JSA) on August 18, 1976. A team of South Korean workers, escorted by UN Command troops, was ordered to trim a poplar tree near the Bridge of No Return, as the tree was blocking the line of sight between a UN checkpoint and a UN observation post. North Korean troops objected and sent a team to stop them. When their objections were ignored, the North Koreans attacked the UN troops with axes dropped by the South Korean workers, killing two US officers.

The UN responded on August 21 with Operation Paul Bunyan, a massive show of force. Named for the mythical American lumberjack, the operation

North Korean troops attack US and South Korean troops in the Axe Murder Incident of Aug 18, 1976. (left)
US troops cut down a poplar tree as part of Operation Paul Bunyan. (right)

was, in essence, a tree-cutting operation, albeit one conducted by a task force of 813 men, including South Korean special forces, and backed up by helicopters, fighter jets, B-52 bombers, and a US aircraft carrier parked off the Korean coast. The task force took 42 minutes to cut down the poplar tree as the North Koreans watched silently.

SOVIET DEFECTOR INCIDENT

On November 23, 1984, Vasily Matusak, a Soviet national on a communist-led tour of the JSA, dashed across the Military Demarcation Line in a bid to defect to the West. The North Koreans pursued, shooting as they did. The UN-led Joint Security Force (JSF) mobilized to protect Matusak and repel the North Koreans. In the ensuing firefight, one South Korean soldier was killed and an American soldier wounded, while three North Koreans were killed and five wounded (another eight were captured). A negotiated ceasefire allowed the North Koreans to withdraw.

2

Chapter Two

THE KOREAN WAR

To understand the DMZ, one must first understand the Korean War, the tragedy that brought the DMZ into existence. Frequently called "the Forgotten War" in the West, largely thanks to its timing between World War II and the Vietnam War, the war was nevertheless a historical event that changed the course of modern world. Columbia University professor Robert Jervis wrote that "the Korean War shaped the course of the cold war....without Korea, international history would have been very different."[*]

The Korean War was the true start of the Cold War, which had been building up in the years immediately after World War II. The war led to a worsening of tensions between the Western camp, mostly capitalist democracies led by the United States, and the

[*] "The Impact of the Korean War on the Cold War," *Journal of Conflict Resolution,* December 1980, Vol. 24, No. 4, 563-592

communist camp, led by the Soviet Union, which in turn led to spiraling arms races and the polarization of global politics. The Korean War also left the superpowers with the impression that it would be the last war fought with conventional weapons, spurring efforts by the US and Soviet Union to develop their nuclear arsenals and opening the door to the Nuclear Age.

It may be called "forgotten" in the West, but the war is anything but forgotten in Korea, where the scars inflicted by the brutal conflict are still readily apparent, the pain never far from the surface. The war pitted Korean against Korean and left countless people dead and maimed, homes and factories destroyed, families separated, and a nation divided in bitter enmity.

Statue in front of the War Memorial of Korea in Seoul.

PRELUDE TO THE WAR

The Korean War began on the morning of June 25, 1950, when North Korean forces poured over the 38th Parallel in a blitzkrieg attack on South Korea, but the war's roots were planted long before that tragic day. The 35-year colonial occupation by the Japanese (1910-1945) traumatized Korean society greatly, as imperial exploitation intensified ideological divisions. After Liberation, these divisions led to the establishment of separate North and South Korean governments, which in turn led to the outbreak of the Korean War.

Japanese Occupation

After a period of isolation, Korea opened up to Western trade at the end of the 19th century. Faced with pressures from ambitious neighbors, Korea made an effort to modernize, but circumstances were not favorable. Following Japan's victories in the First Sino-Japanese War (1894-1895) and Russo-Japanese War (1904-1905), Tokyo acted with virtual impunity in Korea. Japan's efforts to bring Korea under its control culminated with Tokyo's official annexation of Korea in 1910.

For the next 35 years, Korea served as both a springboard for further Japanese aggression on the Asian mainland and a subject of exploitation in its own right. Japanese rule in Korea proved harsh: nationalist protests were crushed with exemplary brutality. Japanese settlers flocked to Korea, gaining a stranglehold on the colony's economy. Discrimination was widespread, particularly in education and economic activities. The colonial authorities even endeavored to "Japanify" the population by denigrating Koreans' culture and ethnic identity.

Under Japanese rule, many Korean resources were utilized for Japan. Japanese land reform did away with Korea's traditional land ownership system, in the process turning countless Korean peasants into tenant farmers. Some wealthy landlords and the emerging capitalist class largely collaborated with this and benefited as a result. Japanese infrastructural developments, including railroads, harbors, and irrigation and land reclamation projects, opened up opportunities for business and trade but required the large-scale exploitation of Korean labor. The railroads and harbors also made it easier for the Japanese to exploit the colony economically: Korean rice flowed from the country to feed Japan's hungry factory workers even while Koreans' per capita rice consumption declined.

Many intellectuals were distressed by the miserable conditions of farmers and laborers and objected to Japan's culturally destructive policies. Tenant farmers, deprived of rights to the land they'd farmed for generations, were forced to turn over much of their harvest as rent; destitute, many chose to emigrate to Manchuria or Japan. Industrial laborers agitated against exploitation. Disgusted with Japanese imperialism and capitalist exploitation, some turned to left-wing ideologies like socialism and communism.

Seoul headquarters of the Oriental Development Company, imperial Japan's answer to the British East India Company and a tool of exploitation in colonial Korea.

In the 1930s, as Japan's war in China worsened and militarists took control in Tokyo, Japanese exploitation of Korea worsened. Things worsened still in the lead-up to the Pacific War as Korean laborers, forcefully mobilized to support the Japanese war effort, were sent to factories and mines in Korea, Manchuria, and Japan,

TIMELINE: BEFORE THE WAR

Nov 22-25 Cairo Conference declares that "in due course Korea shall become free and independent."

Aug 22 Japan forcefully annexes Korea.

1943

1910

Jul 17-Aug 2 Potsdam Conference deals only briefly with Korea.

1945

Aug 15 Japan surrenders to the Allies.

Sept 2 Supreme Commander of the Allied Powers decides to divide Korea into Soviet and American zones of occupation at the 38th Parallel.

Dec 28 Moscow Conference proposes a five-year trusteeship over Korea.

where they frequently worked in dangerous conditions and received poor treatment. Drafted Korean soldiers were sent to die at the front lines, while Korean women were even forced into prostitution to service the Japanese army.

Issue of Korea submitted to UN General Assembly.

US troops complete their withdrawal from Korea.

○ ○○ ○ ○ ○○

The Republic of Korea (South Korea) is established.

The Democratic People's Republic of Korea (North Korea) is established.

UN General Assembly recognizes the Republic of Korea as the only legal government of Korea.

US Secretary of State Dean Acheson does not include South Korea in a speech delineating the American defense line in East Asia.

North Korea invades South Korea along the entire 38th Parallel.

Liberation and National Division

The surrender of Imperial Japan to the Allies on August 15, 1945 brought an end to the Second World War, and with it an end to Japanese rule in Korea. This did not mean immediate independence for Korea, however. Meeting in Cairo in November 1943, the leaders of the United States, Great Britain, and China declared that after Japan's defeat, Korea would gain its independence in "due course." In August 1945, as Japan's defeat grew imminent, Soviet forces swept into Manchuria. Fearing the Soviets would occupy the whole of Korea, threatening the soon-to-be-launched American occupation of Japan, the Americans proposed on August 10 the division of Korea into two zones of occupation, one Soviet and the other American. Without consulting with Korea experts, let alone Koreans themselves, two US Army officers chose the 38th Parallel as the line of division (see p16). The Soviets accepted. Red Army troops moved into northern Korea, soon to be followed in southern Korea by the Americans, who landed at Incheon on September 8, 1945.

The division of Korea was initially meant to be a temporary measure, a mere military convenience to accept the surrender of Japanese troops. Distrust between the West and the Soviets, however, soon gave birth to the Cold War, and the temporary

Inauguration of South Korea's first president, Rhee Syngman, on Aug 15, 1948.

division took on a look of permanence, much as it did in Germany.

In the North, the Soviets put in power communist, pro-Soviet figures such as communist partisan Kim Il-sung. Former collaborators with the Japanese and non-communist nationalists were supressed. Industries were nationalized and land redistributed.

In the American zone of occupation, things were very different. Southern Korea's US military rulers, needing skilled manpower, kept in office officials who collaborated with the Japanese. They failed to carry out land reform, bitterly disappointing those who had hoped the end of Japanese rule would also end their own exploitation. This led to protests, anger, and, later, uprisings and guerrilla war as the discontented increasingly saw communism as their salvation.

Attempts by the Americans and Soviets to form a united Korean government failed, and in 1947 the US brought the issue of Korea before the United Nations, a move opposed by Moscow. On November 14, the UN, despite a Soviet boycott, passed a resolution calling for free elections to be held and foreign troops withdrawn. To oversee the elections, the United Nations Temporary Commission on Korea was created.

Soviet opposition continued, however, and on May 10, 1948, a UN-supervised general election was conducted, but only in the US-occupied south; the Soviets boycotted the vote in the north. A parliament was formed, a constitution written, and on August 15, the Republic of Korea (South Korea) was declared, with pro-American independence activist Syngman Rhee as the first president. A little later, on September 9, the Democratic People's Republic of Korea (North Korea) was declared in the north, with Kim Il-sung as premier. Soviet and American troops were soon withdrawn from the Korean Peninsula. Neither regime recognized the other, and along the 38th Parallel, the two sides engaged in a series of bloody clashes. At the same time, the South, struggling to deal with the social legacy of colonialism, contended with internal instability and violent uprisings.

FRATRICIDAL WAR

The Outbreak of the War

The hostility between North and South finally erupted into full-scale warfare on the morning of June 25, 1950, when North Korean troops poured across the 38th Parallel into South Korea. The North Koreans were well armed with Soviet tanks and artillery; its army also included battle-hardened veterans of the recently concluded Chinese Civil War, in which many Korean communists had fought. The South Korean army, on the other hand, was woefully unprepared for the surprise invasion. The South Korean capital of Seoul fell in three days, and President Syngman Rhee—who once boisterously talked of marching north to reunify the country—fled south with his government.

The UN immediately condemned the invasion, and on June 27 the UN Security Council passed Resolution 83, calling on UN member nations to furnish assistance to South Korea. Some 16 nations eventually did. The US responded almost immediately, providing naval and air support and moving troops from Japan to

Korea. Like the South Koreans, however, the Americans were woefully unprepared for war. In the first encounter between American and North Korean forces in the war, the Battle of Osan (July 5), North Korean forces easily overran a small American task force. The

US bombers destroy warehouses and docks at the strategic port of Wonsan, North Korea, in 1951.

North Koreans continued to push the Americans and South Koreans back, defeating the US 24th Infantry Division in the Battle of Daejeon and capturing the division's commanding general in the victory. By September, the South Koreans and Americans were confined to a small perimeter surrounding the southeastern port city of Busan. It appeared that the North Koreans were on the verge of uniting the Korean Peninsula by force of arms.

Incheon Landing

The Americans and South Koreans held, however, blunting North Korean attempts to break the Busan Perimeter. Behind the perimeter, the Americans and other UN allies built up their forces, waiting for their chance to go on the offensive. They got it on September 15, when the US 1st Marine Division and 7th Infantry Division and South Korean troops and marines successfully executed the Incheon Landing, an amphibious assault deep behind enemy lines that was planned by UN Commander Gen. Douglas MacArthur. Soon after, UN and South Korean troops broke out of the Busan Perimeter, driving north. Cut off, surrounded, and battered from the brutal fighting along the Busan Perimeter, the North Koreans fled north; some made it, while many were killed or captured or went into the mountains to fight as partisans. On September 28, UN forces recaptured the South Korean capital of Seoul.

Ignoring the 38th Parallel, the pre-war line of division, the UN

Gen. MacArthur, Commander in Chief of UN Forces, and his staff observe the shelling of Incheon on Sept 15, 1950.

forces, including South Korea, crossed into North Korea, pursuing the fleeing communist army. On October 19, US and South Korean troops captured the North Korean capital of Pyongyang. UN troop elements even briefly reached the Amnokgang (Yalu) River, the border between North Korea and China, on November 21. Once on the verge of defeat, the UN now appeared on the verge of uniting the Korean Peninsula under South Korean rule.

TIMELINE: DURING THE WAR

1950

JUN 25 North Korea invades South Korea along the entire 38th Parallel.

JUN 25 UN Security Council adopts resolution calling for North Korea to terminate hostilities immediately and withdraw.

JUN 28 North Korean troops enter downtown Seoul.

AUG 3 Bridges over the Nakdonggang River blown, Busan Perimeter established.

SEPT 15 Incheon Landing

SEPT 28 UN troops retake Seoul.

OCT 19 UN forces capture Pyongyang.

OCT 25 Entering the Korean War, Communist Chinese forces launch their first offensive.

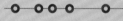

1951

JAN 4 UN troops abandon Seoul as Chinese forces advance.

MAR 19 UN troops launch counteroffensive along the entire front, driving the Chinese back.

JUL 10 Armistice talks begin in Gaeseong.

SEPT 30 US 1st Marine Division fights Battle of the Punchbowl.

Chinese Involvement

It was not to be. Worried about the approach of US troops to its border, the People's Republic of China began secretly moving a massive force into North Korea in October. On October 25, they launched their first offensive, decimating South Korean and US troops in surprise attacks and knocking the UN back to the Cheongcheongang River. The Chinese unexpectedly retreated, and

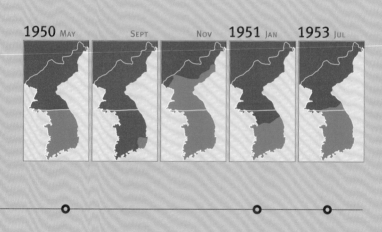

1950 MAY   SEPT   NOV   **1951** JAN   **1953** JUL

1952   FEB 18 Riots at UN-run prison camp on Geoje Island leave 60 North Korean and Chinese prisoners and one US soldier dead.

1953   APR 20 Wounded prisoners exchanged at Panmunjeom.

JUL 27 Armistice signed. Ceasefire goes into effect along the front from 10 pm.

the Americans—disastrously misjudging Chinese intentions—continued their drive north, promising to end the war by Christmas. On November 24, the Chinese launched a second surprise offensive, ambushing and annihilating UN forces and prompting the longest retreat in US Army history. The Chinese and regrouped North Koreans forced UN forces out of North Korea and re-invaded the South, recapturing Seoul on January 4, 1951.

Demoralized by the retreat, the US 8th Army solidified with the arrival of its new commander, the charismatic Gen. Matthew Ridgeway. At the Battle of Jipyeong-ri (Feb 13-15), US and French troops finally blunted the Chinese offensive. UN forces went on the offensive again, recapturing Seoul on March 14. In April and May, the Chinese launched their final major offensives of the war and would have recaptured Seoul if not for heroic defensive actions by UN forces, particularly by British, Canadian, and Australian troops. At the end of May, the UN counterattacked: in the mountainous

16 NATIONS THAT FOUGHT UNDER UN FLAG

US	1,789,000		Turkey	14,936
UK	56,000		Thailand	6,326
Australia	8,407		Greece	4,992
Netherlands	5,322		South Africa	826
Canada	25,687		Belgium	3,498
New Zealand	3,794		Luxembourg	83
France	3,421		Colombia	5,100
Philippines	7,420		Ethiopia	3,518

• Countries That Provided Medical Support

Sweden	160	Norway	623	Denmark	630
India	627	Italy	128		

(Source: Institute for Military History Compilation)

Memorial to the French troops who fought at the Battle of Jipyeong-ri, a major turning point of the war.

central and eastern regions, it drove across the 38th Parallel to seize positions in the heavily fortified "Iron Triangle" and "Punchbowl" regions.

Fiercest Battles

By July, the front lines had grown more or less static, and on July 10 talks for an armistice to end the fighting began. Thus began perhaps the cruelest part of the Korean War. It took a full two years to hammer out an armistice. In the meantime, the armies continued to fight. Some of the bloodiest battles of the war were fought in this period. Little territory was ever exchanged, however: battles, while brutal, were always fought for limited objectives, mostly for strategic hilltops. In the Battle of White Horse Hill (Oct 6-15, 1952), for instance, South Korean troops suffered some 4,000 casualties to seize a hilltop that changed hands 24 times in the ten-day battle. In the Second Battle of Pork Chop Hill, waged just a week before the Armistice was signed, the Americans and Chinese lost 243 and 1,500 men, respectively, in a battle over a hilltop of limited strategic value.

On July 27, 1953, the North Koreans, Chinese, and UN Command signed a ceasefire agreement at the front-line village of Panmunjeom. The South Koreans, who objected to the agreement, refused to sign, but obeyed the ceasefire regardless. Both sides pulled back two kilometers from the front line, giving birth to the Korean Demilitarized Zone. The Korean War was over.

MILITARY CASUALTIES

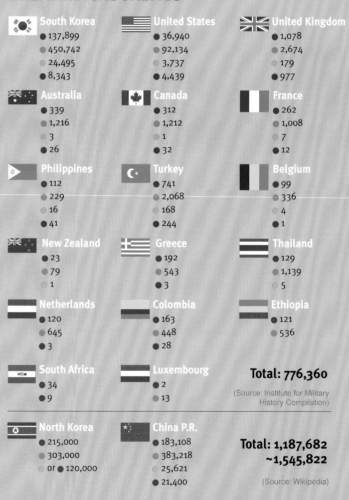

South Korea
- 137,899
- 450,742
- 24,495
- 8,343

United States
- 36,940
- 92,134
- 3,737
- 4,439

United Kingdom
- 1,078
- 2,674
- 179
- 977

Australia
- 339
- 1,216
- 3
- 26

Canada
- 312
- 1,212
- 1
- 32

France
- 262
- 1,008
- 7
- 12

Philippines
- 112
- 229
- 16
- 41

Turkey
- 741
- 2,068
- 168
- 244

Belgium
- 99
- 336
- 4
- 1

New Zealand
- 23
- 79
- 1

Greece
- 192
- 543
- 3

Thailand
- 129
- 1,139
- 5

Netherlands
- 120
- 645
- 3

Colombia
- 163
- 448
- 28

Ethiopia
- 121
- 536

South Africa
- 34
- 9

Luxembourg
- 2
- 13

Total: 776,360

(Source: Institute for Military History Compilation)

North Korea
- 215,000
- 303,000
- or 120,000

China P.R.
- 183,108
- 383,218
- 25,621
- 21,400

Total: 1,187,682
~1,545,822

(Source: Wikipedia)

● Killed in action ● Wounded in action ● Missing in action ● POW

IMPACT OF THE KOREAN WAR

South Korea

South Korea suffered greatly due to the war. According to the South Korean Ministry of Defense, the South Korean military took over 620,000 casualties, including almost 138,000 dead. Even more heartbreaking was the civilian casualty count: over 990,000 South Koreans were killed, injured, or dragged to the North, or disappeared during the war. Some 3.2 million Koreans became refugees, another 300,000 fled the country, and about 100,000 children were made orphaned.

Economically, South Korea was devastated by the war, with much of the country's industrial and transportation infrastructure in ruins. The severing of north-south rail and road links had a further debilitating effect, as did the loss of much of Korea's pre-war energy production, which was located in the North. Not surprisingly, South Korea spent much of the immediate post-war period highly dependent on foreign aid as it tried to rebuild from the devastation. The war, and the constant North Korean threat afterwards, necessitated a strong alliance between South Korea and the US and well as a long-term US troop

Post-war economic prosperity: the COEX in Seoul

commitment that continues to this day.

Beginning in the 1960s, the Korean economy would enter a period of unprecedented economic growth, but the effects of the war continued to be felt. Due to the North Korean threat, the military and anti-communism were facts of South Korean life. This included coups in 1961 and 1979 and several decades of military rule. South Korea transitioned to a full democracy in 1987, but the social and cultural impact of Korea's post-war militarization has continued to linger.

North Korea

Reliable statistics are hard to come by in the case of North Korea, but there is no doubt that the country was devastated by the war. Constant bombing by UN air forces left North Korea's cities and factories in ruins. The South Korean Ministry of Defense estimates that North Korea suffered 1.5 million civilian casualties during the war.

Goose-stepping North Korean soldiers on parade.

As was the case with South Korea, the war left North Korea highly militarized. Even today, the North Korean military establishment is one of the largest in the world and receives a high proportion of North Korea's budget. The country is almost permanently on a war footing, resulting in a highly disciplined and controlled society. The centralization and militarization are largely responsible for the severe economic problems suffered by North Korea from the early 1990s.

The United States

The United States drastically cut its military spending after World War II and reduced the size of its armed forces in preparation for the coming peace. The Korean War changed all this. Unprepared for war, US forces performed badly in the opening stage of the Korean War and were nearly driven from the peninsula. In response, the US boosted its defense spending and practically doubled the size of its army and air force.

More importantly, the Korean War focused American attention on the Communist threat, and so could be considered the real start of the Cold War. US security commitments to Europe and Asia—backed by overseas deployments of US troops—were made and/or strengthened, the most important of these being the NATO alliance in Western Europe. The US also began taking an active role in containing communism in the Third World, most notably in Vietnam.

The Soviet Union

The Korean War was something of a disaster for the Soviet Union; not only did North Korean leader Kim Il-sung fail to unify the Korean Peninsula, but the war brought Western Europe, Japan, and the anti-communist states of Asia closer together. The war did bring the Soviet Union and China closer togetheras well, but it also exposed rifts that would shortly develop into the Sino-Soviet split.

China

The butcher's bill for China was truly horrifying. Official Chinese sources claim 114,000 killed and 380,000 wounded. US sources, however, claim the Chinese death toll to be over 400,000, with 486,000 wounded. While Chinese forces experienced early success, their weaknesses in firepower, air support, and logistics soon became painfully obvious. After the war, China began a push to modernize and professionalize its military, a major departure from its previous military doctrine that prioritized ideology over expertise and technology.

The war also led to a period of hostility between China and the US. Not only did the arms of the two nations meet in Korea, but the US also moved to put Taiwan under its protection, preventing China from conquering the island. Chinese relations with the US remained frosty until US President Richard Nixon's 1972 trip to China.

Japan

While Japan, then under US occupation, was not a direct party to the war, the war nevertheless had a great impact on the country, and particularly its economy. Japanese companies made a killing supplying the US war effort; what's more, in the eyes of the Americans, Japan's large conglomerates went from foe to friend.

The war also forced the Americans to rethink their policies with regard to Japanese security, especially as forces previously based in Japan were redeployed to Korea. Gradually, Japan was allowed to remilitarize. When in 1951 Japan signed the San Francisco Treaty, the peace treaty that officially ended World War II, it also signed a security treaty with the US that would, in 1960, become the Treaty of Mutual Cooperation and Security between the US and Japan.

Chapter Three

PANMUNJEOM AND THE JSA

> *"It's one bad place, but it's also a huge tourist draw. Every year, about 180,000 tourists are bused up from Seoul, 30 miles to the south, to spend a day in the clean air and wide open spaces of the last flashpoint of the Cold War. Think of it as Dangerland, a bizarre theme park to cataclysmic mass death."*

"Borderline Absurdity: A Fun-Filled Tour of the Korean DMZ,"
Washington Post, Jan 11, 1998

The most iconic image of the DMZ is the Joint Security Area (JSA), frequently—albeit incorrectly—referred to as Panmunjeom. Bisected by the Military Demarcation Line, the JSA is the only place in the DMZ where South Korean and North Korean soldiers come face to face. The tensions here are palpable: everyone, military and civilian alike, follows a strict code of behavior, and incidents in the JSA, while rare, have resulted in the deaths of South Korea, American, and North Korean personnel. Like Checkpoint

Charlie in Berlin, it was—and still is—a dramatic symbol of the Cold War, although one not without its irony: despite, or perhaps because of, the tense atmosphere, the JSA is one of Korea's most popular tourist destinations, drawing bus loads of curious visitors ever day.

PANMUNJEOM

First things first: popular media parlance to the contrary, Panmunjeom and the JSA are two separate places.

Located 53 km to the northwest of Seoul, the village of Panmunjeom was nothing more than a wayside village on the road linking the South Korean capital with the important provincial town of Gaeseong. Prior to the war, it was called Neolmun-ri, a

purely Korean term that means "village of the wooden gate." It is said that many years ago, the Korean king was passing through the village. He wished to cross the Sacheon Stream, which flows nearby, but found himself unable to as there was no bridge. Moving to rectify this, local villagers removed the wooden gates of their homes and used the wood to build a bridge for the king.

In 1951, however, it was just a nondescript handful of Korean mud huts and a traditional inn for travelers. It did have two things

South and North Korean soldiers glare at one another in the JSA.

going for it, though: it was on the road to Gaeseong, and it was located close to the front lines, but not close enough to be at risk. This made a rather attractive location when, in October 1951, the UN Command was looking for a safer, more neutral area to hold armistice talks (see p48), which since July had been conducted in the communist-held city of Gaeseong.

On October 7, the communists agreed to transfer the venue for the armistice talks from Gaeseong to Neolmun-ri, which now came to be called by the Sino-Korean pronunciation of its name, Panmunjeom, as a courtesy to the Chinese delegation. Three-mile neutral zones were also declared over the nearby towns of Gaeseong and Munsan (site of the UN base camp for the talks). Soon, the mud huts were joined by a tent "truce village" to host the talks. Of course, Panmunjeom had plenty of time to become famous: the interminable armistice talks dragged on for nearly two years before the two sides, battered and bloody, finally agreed to a ceasefire on July 27, 1953.

Today, the village of Panmunjeom has practically disappeared. All that remains is the pavilion where the Korean Armistice was signed, preserved as a museum by the North Koreans. Shortly after the Armistice was signed, however, a new neutral venue for further negotiations was built about 1 km away; this became the JSA.

Panmunjeom in early period.
Photo from *Korean War in Color* by John Rich.

On 24 October a fleet of nine 2 1/2 ton trucks moved out of Munsan-ni and crossed the Imjin River. Loaded with tents and equipment the convoy rolled into the tiny village of Panmunjom and its cluster of mud huts. Swiftly the tent city to house the conferees rose and a crew of forty men worked intently to install the flooring, lighting, and heating that the approach of cold weather now made necessary. By the following day the new site was ready.

The main conference area had several large tents set aside for joint use and three that were to be at the disposal of the UNC delegates and the press. Half a mile south the service echelons set up the mess, communications, security, and engineer facilities that would support the negotiations and aid in neutralizing the truce conference area. Overnight, Panmunjom became famous.

Walter G. Hermes, *Truce Tent and Fighting Front*, Chapter VI

THE ARMISTICE TALKS

Negotiations for an armistice began on July 10, 1951. The talks proved more painful than anyone could have imagined: they dragged on for two years and 18 days, requiring 1,076 meetings, many of them nasty and arduous. All the while, the two sides' armies continued to slaughter one another in the field, although, frustratingly, neither side attempted to seize much territory, instead preferring to butcher men to capture limited objectives of questionable strategic value like hilltop observation posts.

The first armistice talks were convened in Gaeseong, an ancient Korean city that, prior to the war, had been South Korean, but as of 1951 was controlled by the Chinese and North Koreans. A series of incidents, however, prompted the UN to request the talks be moved to the more neutral site of Panmunjeom, a request accepted by the North Koreans on Oct 7, 1951.

Issue of the Border

The first UN troops to cross the 38th Parallel hold a sign posting ceremony.

The talks were conducted by teams composed of five military delegates, who in turn were assisted by staff officers. The UN team was led by Vice Admiral C. Turner Joy, Commander of the US Naval Forces Far East until May 1952, when he was replaced by Lt. Gen. William K. Harrison, Jr. The Chinese/North Korean side was led by Lt. Gen. Nam Il, chief of staff of the North Korean Army.

The talks frequently proved difficult and bitter, sometimes descending into posturing and insults. First there was the issue of the border. The communists preferred to revert to the pre-war border of the 38th Parallel. The UN, on the other hand, wished to draw the border along the military front line, giving South Korea control of strategic territory north of the 38th Parallel in mountainous central and western Korea. Eventually, the communist side agreed to follow the military front line; it is this line that the DMZ follows today.

POWs

More contentious, however, was the issue of prisoners of war. UN forces had taken countless North Korean and Chinese prisoners. Many of these North Koreans were, in fact, South Koreans drafted into the North Korean Army, while many of the Chinese prisoners were captured members of the Kuomintang Army. Given a choice, these prisoners would choose to remain in South Korea or go to Taiwan. In fact, UN screening revealed that only 70,000 of 170,000 Chinese and North Korean prisoners wanted to be repatriated. The United States was very reluctant to send anyone back against his will. This ran against the Geneva Convention, however, which stipulated that the POWs be returned home. The two sides eventually agreed to allow a Neutral Nations Repatriation Commission to handle the POW repatriation issue.

Finally, there was the issue of South Korea. Led by the nationalist and fiercely anti-communist Rhee Syngman, South Korea opposed the armistice talks, preferring instead for the UN to continue the war to complete victory. On June 17, Rhee unilaterally released all Korean POWs held in UN camps, outraging the North Koreans and Chinese and bringing the talks to a halt. The communists refused to sign an armistice until the UN could guarantee South Korea would abide by it. This the UN managed to do, the US winning Rhee's cooperation with a package of security guarantees and aid.

At 10 am, on July 27, 1953, Nam and Harrison signed the Korean Armistice. The document was soon after countersigned by UN Commander Gen. Mark

Clark, Chinese commander Peng Dehuai, and North Korean leader Kim Il-sung in separate ceremonies in Munsan and Gaeseong. The Korean War was over.

Patients are carried on a Chinese litter from a C-54 air evacuation plane to a waiting ambulance following a flight from Korea.

THE JOINT SECURITY AREA

The Joint Security Area (JSA) was established soon after the signing of the Armistice as a neutral zone for the holding of peace talks. Located about 800 meters south of Panmunjeom (or at least where the village used to be), it is frequently referred to as "Panmunjeom," although this is incorrect.

The JSA is a roughly 800 meter wide area bisected by the Military Demarcation Line. It is home to the Military Armistice Commission (MAC), the agency created by the Armistice to oversee the implementation of the truce. It is also home to a number of pavilions, meeting halls, and checkpoints, some of which have become iconic.

The JSA is guarded by UN and North Korean military police. Neither side can have more than 35 military police on guard at any time. Guarding the UN side is the United Nations Command

North Korea's Stalinist Panmungak Pavilion looms over the JSA.

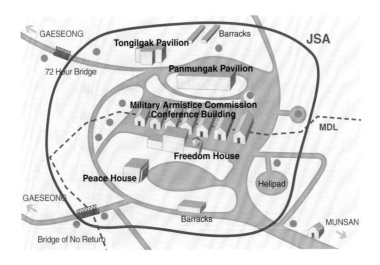

Security Battalion—Joint Security Area. While it was originally manned by an all-American force, an all-South Korean battalion assumed responsibility for the JSA in 2004. To serve at the JSA, South Korean military police must be at least 177 cm tall and hold a black belt in taekwondo or judo. They are armed with pistols, and while on duty they stand in a modified taekwondo stance with stolid facial expressions and sunglasses. It's all very intimidating.

Until 1974, personnel from both sides were able to move about freely within the entire JSA. Following the Axe Murder Incident of that year, however (see p22), the MDL came to be enforced in the JSA as well, meaning that UN and North Korea personnel now keep to their respective sides.

The most interesting building here is the Military Armistice Commission Conference Building, a simple one-story hall painted UN blue. The building is actually bisected by the MDL; inside, however, you are free to cross the line, meaning that this is the only place where visitors may freely move between North and South Korea. The building is supposed to hold meetings of the MAC, but the North Koreans have boycotted the commission since 1998, when a South Korean general was named the top UN negotiator.

On the southern side of the MDL are the impressive Freedom House and Peace House, which, aside from being splendid pieces of modern Korean architecture, are also used—during better periods in

inter-Korean relations—for inter-Korean meetings. On the northern side of the MDL is the Panmungak, a gray Stalinist structure that serves as a North Korean waiting room and office for North Korean guards.

One of the more poignant places in the JSA is the Bridge of No Return, a simple concrete bridge that, like the Military Armistice Commission Conference Building, is bisected by the MDL. It earned

An overhead view of the JSA.

South Korean MP

its name after the Armistice, as POWs who elected to go North walked across the bridge to North Korea, never to return. It was at this bridge, too, that the Axe Murder Incident took place (see p22).

Just in front of the JSA on the UN side is Camp Bonifas (named after the US officer axed to death in the JSA in 1974), a large South Korean military installation that serves as the base camp of the United Nations Command Security Force—Joint Security Area. At the camp, visitors will be briefed (usually by a US officer) on the

history and regulations of the JSA. You can also check out the short par-three, one-hole golf course on the base premises—just don't expect to retrieve your golf balls, as the roughs are mine fields. This was described by one golfing journal as the "most dangerous golf course on Earth."

1. World's most dangerous golf course at Camp Bonifas.

2. Old Freedom House, southern side of the JSA.

3. North Korean soldier watches activity on southern side of the JSA.

Chapter Four

HOME TO NATURE EVOLVING

Since the DMZ has remained a no-man's-land for a half century, many people have wondered: "What has been happening within this belt?" The kind of weaponry and the number of soldiers that might be deployed along the DMZ are confidential information involving national security. But one is free to imagine the state of nature within the zone: tall grass and trees thriving in lush splendor, birds and fish reveling in unrestricted freedom, and all manner of wildlife flourishing in this haven, safe from their most feared enemy—human beings. The DMZ and the Civilian Control Line were not established for the benefit of nature, but to deter war. Yet the two zones have effectively prohibited humans from interfering with the nature within. One might imagine Mother Nature thinking, "Humans brought destruction upon themselves by engaging in war, and they are now trying to make up for this damage by letting nature be, shielding it against even the slightest human intervention."

DMZ UNDER STRESS?

Contrary to popular belief, however, this is mostly fantasy. A primitive, virgin forest untouched by human hands does not exist in the DMZ. An intriguing fact is that the DMZ's natural environment does not seem to be aging. The trees may actually be shrinking in some places. In other places, where there used to be valleys teeming with rare species of fish such as *Oncorhynchus masou ishikawae* and *Moroco kumgangensis* (Uchida), the species of fish have vanished. One ecologist noted, "Ecological succession is constantly taking place within the DMZ, or else the succession process itself suffers from interference." The forests in the DMZ and in the surrounding areas existed as disclimax forests where ecological succession had been interrupted. That is to say, something has seriously disrupted nature's natural process by causing it stress. But exactly who or what?

Ecological arboretum on the slopes of Mt. Daeamsan in Yanggu. The arboretum, located on about 200 km² of land along the DMZ, is home to many of the rare species of plants found in the zone.

Devastation by the War

First of all, the forests in the DMZ suffered much from the ravages of war. People used to live in the vicinity of the DMZ before the outbreak of the Korean War; within the zone, there were some 70 villages. These were mostly farming communities that utilized traditional Korean farming methods to cultivate farmland not only in the fields and valleys but alongside mountain slopes as well. The trees in the forests near the villages also provided a ready supply of fuel for Korea's traditional under-floor heating system. Then the Korean War proceeded to destroy the natural environment of the area with wanton violence. The war lasted 37 months and two days. The DMZ was the battleground for two-thirds of the fighting during the war, which extensively devastated the area's forests and farmlands. Moreover, the DMZ battles were characterized by each side fighting fiercely to gain control of the highlands or mountain areas. Due to this battlefield tactic, the animals living in the forests on the slopes of mountains were all sacrificed, and even the trees and animals that escaped from direct harm ended up with a totally devastated habitat. The war left both nature and people thoroughly spent. The natural environment of the DMZ was seriously wounded, but it somehow managed to survive the war. It takes 150 to 200 years for devastated forests in temperate zones to develop into climax forests. The environment of the DMZ, extensively laid waste to by war, was comparable to a patient lying in the ICU after undergoing life-threatening surgery.

Overpopulation

Second, a surprisingly high population density is affecting the environmental conditions of the DMZ. It is a mistake to equate the population of the areas around the DMZ with the officially announced numbers. Since disclosing the actual number of soldiers deployed near the border would be detrimental to national security,

North Korean observation point in the DMZ. A considerable number of soldiers operate within the zone.

troops are regarded as a "hidden population." The county of Hwacheon in Gangwon-do Province, which measures 909.45 square kilometers in area, borders the DMZ. Population statistics as of the end of 2005 indicated 9,731 households with a population of 23,822 (12,471 male, 11,351 female), and a population density of 26.2 per square kilometer. Although this is the second lowest population density in South Korea, only civilians were counted; it is difficult to know what the actual population, including members of the armed forces, amounts to. But at least one thing is clear—people look at the low population density based on the official population statistics and believe that the natural environment in the DMZ must be far less affected by humans than other areas.

The War Goes On

Third, there is the fact that the war is not yet over in the DMZ. Item 6, Article 1 of the Armistice Agreement stipulates: "Neither side shall execute any hostile act within, from, or against the Demilitarized Zone," but this regulation was rendered useless beginning in 1960. The entire length of the DMZ was turned into a virtual fortress, while the distance between opposing forces gradually narrowed as the two sides started to break their promise to withdraw 2 km from the MDL. In fact, the Demilitarized Zone was actually transformed into a "Heavily Militarized Zone"— another battlefield. This modern-day confrontation also employed a classic military tactic from ancient China that involved burning up all the plant life that could obscure one's vision from mid-February until May of each year. Nineteen fires broke out in the DMZ in 2000 because of this practice, which was responsible for burning 371 square kilometers of forest, or 40 percent of the overall area of the DMZ.

Legacy of Warfare

The two sides have also unleashed "chemical warfare" in this war against trees and plants. The DMZ's environment was subjected to concentrated showers of deadly defoliants, such as Agent Orange, Agent Blue, and Monuron from 1968 to 1969. It is only now that people are gradually awakening to the fact that these chemical agents, which are so lethal that they even shrivel the roots of plant life, must have wreaked tremendous havoc on the DMZ's ecosystem at that time. Not only the people who had been within the DMZ at the time but also their offspring who had never set foot in the zone experienced side effects. It became apparent that the wildlife within the DMZ must have suffered from even more serious consequences.

One can easily imagine the suffering the wild animals must experience due to the land mines in the DMZ, which are estimated to number one million. Whereas humans are aware of the dangers of these mines, innocent animals are certain to be maimed repeatedly by these savage devices of humankind.

Land mine warning sign

Consequently, the environment of the DMZ not only sustained countless wounds during the Korean War but has also continued to suffer from the effects of the Cold War that has persisted for half a century. Tall trees have stopped growing, and burnt forests have been replaced by grassland.

Unintended Deviations

The animals that sought shelter from humans in the forests became victims of land mines, while herbicides afflicted the animals that managed to survive among the mines. In particular, the DMZ's ecosystem has failed to evolve in a natural manner. There is a strong likelihood that the plants and animals there that learned to adapt to the stress of the Cold War

Acacia trees

have since produced entirely new and unintended deviations in the natural ecosystem. It is certain that they are evolving in directions that we have not anticipated, as evidenced by the following examples.

Within the forests, where land mines are scattered about with red warning signs, white flowers resembling butterflies, which give off a heavy aroma, come into full bloom each spring. These are acacia trees (*Robinia pseudoacacia* L.), which were introduced to Korea in the early 20th century to restore wastelands. Despite their various uses, Koreans soon came to loathe acacia trees because their rapid proliferation could quickly crowd out other trees in the area. No one would have gone into the forests of the DMZ to plant these trees—not when countless mines lay in wait for their next victim. As if enjoying the freedom from humans the mines provided, acacia trees soon overtook the forests.

Koreans are not very familiar with hogweed, a creeping perennial herb. The herb originated in North America, but it also thrives in Manchuria. No Korean had ever seen this weed, which grows from 1 to 3 cm a year, before the Korean War. But if each and every hogweed plant growing in the vicinity of the DMZ were counted, one would find that no other plant in Korea has managed to multiply as fruitfully. Research conducted in 2000 by the Gyeonggi Development Institute on the natural ecosystem of the upper estuary of the Hantangang River revealed that the giant hogweed (*Ambrosia trifida L.*) and common hogweed (*Ambrosia artemisiifolia*) comprised the densest communities among the 37 types of tracheophytes growing in the area.

Consider the case of dandelions, the wildflowers that grow along roadsides, where they are often trampled underfoot. These flowers are not usually found at high altitudes. But on the summit of Mt. Daeam-san, which rises 1,300 meters above sea level, there is a sea of dandelions as large as a soccer field. They are tall dandelions of Western origin. Like air borne troops, these flowers have managed to scale their way up to the top of the mountain, where they captured the territory of native alpine flora and built their own kingdom. The DMZ is home to 97 species of foreign origin that immigrated to the nation, including the Chinese chrysanthemum, giant goldenrod (*Solidago serotina Ait.*), annual fleabane (*Erigeron annuus*), and evening primrose.

Free-Falling Black Vultures

Then there are the black vultures. Though they are often called the "lords of the sky," they also are known by the not-so-honorable name of "scavenger" for their penchant for picking over the carcasses of animals and birds. But the black vultures of the DMZ are deserving of another name: "free-falling birds." December 14, 1993, the day that black vultures were sighted in Hwacheon,

Gangwon-do, marked their return to Korea's east coast after a 12-year hiatus. But their debut in the DMZ turned out to be an abysmal failure, as they ended up dehydrated and starved, despite their two-meter wingspan, sharp eyes, piercing beak, and powerful legs and talons. That December, numerous black vultures fell from the sky like stones onto the DMZ, with several exhausted black vultures on the verge of death being discovered in various places.

Vultures near Cheorwon

One farmer, who was driving a tractor in Cheorwon, found a black vulture standing like a traffic cop in the middle of an intersection and carried it back home. At that time, a widespread civic movement for animal protection had already taken root in South Korea. Without exception, these "fallen black vultures" were painstakingly nursed back to health, while dining on chicken, fish, and pork to their hearts' content, and were then returned to the wild. Could they have possibly spread the word about this warm hospitality back in their "kingdom of black vultures"? For some reason, the DMZ has since become one of the most popular stopping-off sites for black vultures that fly in from Mongolia in the winter.

Migratory Birds

In some cases, development projects have attracted migratory birds. In the past, a lake in the Pyeonggang Plateau in North Korea was used to irrigate the plains of Cheorwon. With the division of the

Migratory wild geese

Korean Peninsula, however, the southward flow of the waterway was blocked off. Farmers then remembered a deep valley in the DMZ, which was called Heukdari, or "earthen bridge," in the past. The farmers built a dam resembling an earthen bridge and created a huge lake named Togyo Reservoir and a waterway to the plains. This lake adjoins the DMZ, and civilian access is thus prohibited. Only a handful of people who manage the lake know about its actual appearance and depth. But migratory birds from as far away as Siberia have discovered it. Each winter, the lake serves as a rest stop for geese, mallards, and teals that fly in from northern regions. In the past, migratory geese flew high overhead in a V-shaped formation, without bothering to stop off at the Cheorwon Plain.

AMAZING DISCOVERIES

Undocumented Species Discovered

Despite the abnormal evolution of the environment of the DMZ, ecologists are finding and announcing amazing discoveries. In March 2001, the Korea Forest Research Institute, affiliated with the Korea Forest Service, announced the results of an extensive study. The institute discovered a heretofore undocumented species within the DMZ and its surrounding areas, nine species previously unrecorded in Korea, 88 rare species, 48 special species, and six species designated Natural Monuments—accounting for well over 100 species of animals and plants deserving protection. A type of mushroom previously undiscovered in any other part of the world was discovered on Mt. Geonbongsan on the east coast and featured in *National Geographic*. In addition, a cluster of rare edelweiss was also found growing on Hyangnobong Peak, as well as fireweed (*Epilobium angustifolium*), which had previously been thought to exist only on Mt. Baekdu-san. The existence of the beetle

Wild flowers blooming in the Yongneup moor. (left column) Wood anemone, *Megaleranthis saniculifolia, Anemone raddeana, Heloniopsis koreana* (middle column) *Chrysosplenium grayanum, Caltha palustris var. membranacea, Viola orientalis, Trientalis europaea* (right column) *Corydalis grandicalyx* (B.U. Oh & Y.S. Kim), Dog's-tooth violet, *Pseudostellaria palibiniana, Heloniopsis orientalis var. flavida.*

Chromogeotrupes auratus (Motschulsky), which feeds on the excretion of antelopes or musk deer, was also confirmed, as well as the presence of the autogenous wild iris (*Iris setosa*), previously not known to grow in South Korea.

The results of the five-year study were lauded for their detailed documentation of the natural environment of the DMZ. The report also contains the following note: "Due to the influence of forest fires or the construction of roads for military use, the density of trees growing in the research areas was found to be only half the average in Korea, while there was serious soil erosion in many places. Accordingly, it should be pointed out that protective measures should precede any further studies on the ecology of the entire area of the DMZ and the implementation of preservation measures."

The report confirms that the lush forests that we had imagined do not actually exist in the DMZ. The report also emphasizes two points. First, the 100 or so species of animals and plants deserving of protection are treasures unique to the DMZ that have just barely managed to survive and are at risk of being forever lost as the DMZ undergoes a process of adapting to a new environment. Second, it warns against harboring any "fantasy" about the DMZ's natural ecosystem. Studies on the DMZ's natural environment have been carried out steadily since the Korean Research Institute for Conservation of Nature (predecessor to the current Korean Association for Conservation of Nature) and the US-based Smithsonian Institution conducted a two-year academic study in 1966. Another ten large-scale studies have been undertaken with financial support from the government and various academic institutions. But the report by the Korea Forest Research Institute was the first to sound a warning about the extensive destruction of the DMZ's environment.

Unique Natural Environment

For whatever reason, the scholars who have studied the DMZ's natural ecosystem have seemingly turned a blind eye to its state of devastation. A good example is the wetland area on Mt. Daeryeong-san in the midwest part of the DMZ, which is under the protection of the Ramsar Convention. On the top of this mountain, which rises 1,300 meters above sea level, is a plateau measuring 7.78 acres in area. Before this plateau attracted the interest of scholars, it was called Yongneup, or "dragon swamp." Scholars estimated the swamp to be about 4,500 years old and found that it was home to 23 species of insects, including the *Grapholita demorpha* Oriental fruit moth, the *Pyrocoelia rufa* firefly, and varieties of ladybugs, along with 191 species of plants, such as *Gentiana jamesii*. Wetlands are highly valued for their academic significance because they provide the means to study changes to the natural ecosystem or climate that have occurred over the course of thousands of years. The swamp, a two-

Rare highland moor on Mt. Daeam-san, near the DMZ.

meter thick peat bog, also retains the secrets of the area's natural ecosystem as though recorded on microfilm. But this swamp, regarded as the greatest natural treasure of the DMZ, had already been suffering from almost lethal deterioration for some time when it was registered under the Ramsar Convention on Wetlands on March 28, 1997.

CHOPYEONGDO ISLAND

When you venture into the Civilian Control Zone of the northern Gyeonggi-do town of Paju, you catch sight of impressive views that are rarely seen by regular people. Not far from Haemarucheon, the Imjingang River flows along at its own pace, while the island of Chopyeongdo (see the map on p46) sits in silence, unperturbed by its lack of human contact.

The area along the Imjingang is known for its history of adversity. During the Japanese invasion of the Joseon kingdom in 1592, King Seonjo (r. 1552-1608) passed by this area as he fled the fierce fighting, while Chopyeongdo served as a staging ground for Chinese troops during the Korean War.

Careful observation of a river bank shows that it is covered with a thick layer of sediment, in which the tracks of animals can be seen, but not the footprints of people. The area around Chopyeongdo is a spawning ground for the river puffer and home to some 80 species of freshwater fish, including the indigenous *eoreumchi* (*Hemibarbus mylodon*). Western roe deer and Chinese water deer can also be spotted on occasion. River puffer fishermen make their way upstream to find a good spot to cast their nets. The hushed scenery of the river melds with the season's fresh green leaves, creating an idyllic setting that would be suitable for a gathering of Taoist hermits.

Chopyeongdo is an island of substantial scale, covering some 1.65 million square meters. Being essentially untouched by human hands since the time of the Korean War, it serves as a safe refuge for a large bird population.

ENDANGERED SPECIES OF THE DMZ

Asiatic black bear

While the DMZ is by no means pristine, it is nevertheless home to a surprisingly wide variety of endangered plants and animals. In a 2008 study, the National Institute of Environment Research found 3,029 wild species in area past the Civilian Control Line, including 54 endangered species, roughly 24 percent of the total endangered species in Korea. Ten species are especially endangered, including the red bat, musk deer, otter, golden eagle, whitetailed eagle, and black swan.

The DMZ itself hosts 2,800 varieties of animals and plants, 1,170 vascular plants, 146 endangered species, 83 fish species, and 18 endemic species. It has become renowned as a migration ground for birds, including two of the world's most endangered species, the red-crowned crane and the white-naped crane. Other rare species, such as the Asiatic black bear, have been spotted in the forests. A 2010 study by the National Institute of Environmental Research using video cameras detected Siberian musk deer, which was believed to be extinct in South Korea, and the Amur goral, a mountain goat that resembles an antelope.

Of all the animals that have benefited from the DMZ, it is the crane that is perhaps the most spectacular. Regardless of species, cranes are almost universally threatened. The DMZ has provided a refuge for these beautiful creatures, though: some seven species of crane winter on the DMZ's Cheorwon Plain, including about a third of the world's remaining red-crowned cranes and half the remaining white-naped cranes, two incredibly precious species of bird.

The red-crowned crane is one of the rarest birds in the world. There are believed to be no more than 2,800 birds

Red-crowned cranes

worldwide, mostly in China. It's a rather large bird that stands 140 cm high, white in color save for some black feathers on its wings and neck and the patch of red skin on its head from which the bird earns its name. It breeds in the reeds and wetlands of Manchuria and southeastern Siberia and winters in the tidal flats of Korea and eastern China. There is also another population that lives all year round on Hokkaido in northern Japan.

The bird has played a role in East Asian culture. The birds form lifelong monogamous bonds and so, unsurprisingly, they are seen as symbols of fidelity. They are also symbols of long life, happiness, and

An elk and a white-naped crane feeding in the Cheorwon Plain.

peace. In East Asian lore, the immortals of Taoist legend can often be seen riding the majestic birds. Unfortunately, their beauty has also been their curse: in the 20th century, they were hunted almost to extinction for their beautiful plumage, which was particularly valued in hats.

The white-naped crane, which also winters in Cheorwon, is critically endangered, too, with just 5,000 birds worldwide. They breed in the marshes and steppes of Siberia, northern China, Mongolia, and southeastern Russia and winter in southeast China, Korea, and southern Japan. They're not as tall as the red-crowned crane, but they're nonetheless a big bird, standing 130 cm high. Like other cranes, they form lifelong bonds with their mates.

Aside from the freedom from human activity the DMZ provides, the birds come for another reason. Past the Civilian Control Line in Cheorwon, Gangwon-do is a natural spring that pumps out warm water all year round. This produces a large 5,000 square meter pond that never freezes, even in winter. This provides the perfect wintering habitat for migratory birds like cranes and forms the heart of the Saemtong Migratory Bird's Sanctuary, a winter mecca for Korean bird watchers.

Turning the DMZ into an Ecological Park

The DMZ is home to 2,716 species of wild plants and animals, including 67 endangered species.

The Korean government is pushing a plan that would turn the DMZ and its surrounding areas into a global park symbolizing ecology and peace. The plan is being pushed with the goals of preserving the DMZ's natural environment, building a base of inter-Korean exchange and international peace, and developing a new engine of growth for the era of Korean reunification.

In order to turn the DMZ into a symbol of cooperation, peace, coexistence, and coprosperity, the government plans to develop the areas around the DMZ into an ecology and peace belt and a symbolic space of global peace and cooperation, as well as cultivate low-carbon green growth, build north-south and east-west transportation infrastructure, and develop inter-Korean trade.

First, through turning the area into an ecology and peace belt, the government plans to designate the environmentally precious region into a preservation zone and geo-park. Within the Civilian Control Zone, running from Goseong to Ganghwa, the government will create a web of trekking paths to create an ecology and peace park

Participants in a bike rally on Peace Bicycle Nuri Road pass alongside a mine field in Hwacheon, Gangwon-do.

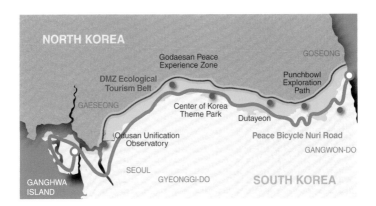

as well as build a unified information system on local ecology, history, and culture.

In order to turn the region into a zone of international peace and cooperation, the government plans to establish a UN Peace University and UN meeting hall in the DMZ and build a specialized hospital for land mine victims in Yanggu.

In Ganghwa, Yeoncheon, Yanggu, Goseong, Cheorwon, Chuncheon, and Hwacheon, the government will create a green growth zone by building clean energy production facilities and high-tech industrial complexes and attracting academic and research facilities.

In order to boost east-west trade in the areas along the DMZ, the government will connect Ganghwa in the west and Goseong in the east with the East-West Green Peace Road, build the West Sea Peace Bridge linking Yeongjong Island and Ganghwa Island, and build transportation infrastructure uniting North and South Korea, as well as restore the existing transportation infrastructure cut after the war. The plan also includes building an inter-Korean cooperation zone in Paju, Cheorwon, and Goseong, as well as a youth exchange center in Yeoncheon.

Chapter Five

THE DMZ
AS A MUSEUM

The Korean Demilitarized Zone may be the world's sole remaining Cold War flashpoint and a unique ecological environment, but it is at the same time a veritable outdoor museum of Korean history. The length of the DMZ is home to countless cultural treasures and heritage sites, including ancient hilltop fortresses, buried palaces, and ruined cities from the Korean War. The iconic Joint Security Area is also one of Korea's most popular tourist destinations, with countless visitors going each year to take in the tension of "living history."

Most of the DMZ's culturally and historically significant sites are open to the public, although some require reservations, while others require you to furnish your own transportation. The added hassle is to be expected, however; the DMZ is, after all, the front line between parties still technically at war. Visits are well worth the trouble, as they allow you to experience in a most tangible way the tragedy of the Korean War and national division.

Unfortunately, the geopolitical situation along the DMZ has hampered research and excavation efforts, and scholars still have very much to learn. It is hoped that as inter-Korean relations improve, however, archaeologists, historians, and preservationists will have further opportunity to conduct work in the hitherto forbidden zone, shedding greater light on Korea's dramatic past.

IMJINGAK

A short train trip north of Seoul brings you to Imjingak, a small park on the broad Imjingang River. A solitary railroad bridge crosses the river; next to it, stand lonely concrete pylons from a bridge long since destroyed. Across the river is the DMZ and, beyond that, North Korea.

For the general visitor, Imjingak is as close to North Korea as you can get without getting special permission. This, combined with its easy access from Seoul, has turned it into a literal shrine to national

Main hall of Imjingak.

division. On the Korean autumn harvest celebration of Chuseok and the Lunar New Year holiday, North Korean-born South Koreans (and their descendants) gather at Imjingak to perform traditional ancestral rites. Other visitors leave colorful ribbons with prayers for peace and reunification.

Imjingak is also home to several war memorials, the Freedom Bridge, and a bullet-scarred train that was bombed near the DMZ in the Korean War.

Mangbaedan Altar

Between 1945, when Korea was divided, and the start of the Korean War, an estimated 3.5 million North Koreans fled to the South to escape communist oppression. They were joined by countless more during the Korean War and, more recently, a growing number of defectors fleeing the famine and repression of

Mangbaedan Altar

1) Visitors look toward the North at Imjingak. 2) Courtyard at Imjingak   3) Peace ribbons on the iron fence at Imjingak. 4) Train destroyed during the Korean War at Imjingak.

today's North Korea. In Korean, these people are called *silhyangmin*, or "people who have lost their hometowns." The first generation of *silhyangmin* have spent the last 60 years without ever setting eyes on the land of their birth, and their plight, one of lost homes and separated families, is one of the enduring tragedies of the Korean War and national division.

In the old days, *silhyangmin* used to come to Imjingak on holidays and construct temporary altars at which they would perform the ancestral rites most Koreans perform in their hometowns. In 1986, however, the South Korean government constructed a permanent altar for their use. The altar consists of an incense burner and seven stone slabs, each one representing a North Korean province. On each slab is carved an image from the province it represents.

Freedom Bridge (foreground) and Imjingang Railway Bridge (background).

Freedom Bridge

Just behind the Mangbaedan Altar is a simple wooden bridge. This bridge, the so-called "Freedom Bridge," was a temporary span built over the Imjingang River in 1953 to carry home some 12,773 South Korean POWs following the Armistice Agreement. It was later moved to its current spot to preserve it as a memorial. At the northern end of the bridge is a barbed wire fence overlooked by a guard tower. This is where the Civilian Control Line begins. Visitors often leave ribbons, banners, and flags on the fence.

The Third Tunnel of Aggression

One of the more popular tourist sites on the DMZ is the so-called Third Tunnel of Aggression, located about half a kilometer south of the Southern Demarcation Line, not far from Panmunjeom. Some

two meters in height, two meters wide, 1,635 meters long, and 73 meters deep, the tunnel was built by the North Koreans to facilitate an invasion of the South: 30,000 men with light weapons could pass through the tunnel into South Korea. It was discovered by the South Koreans in 1978 based on a tip from a North Korean defector.

While at first denying it dug the tunnel, North Korea later admitted to its construction but said it was part of a coal mine. The local geology, however, makes this explanation unlikely. The tunnel is now heavily guarded by the South, but it is still a popular tourist attraction as a symbol of the ongoing tensions along the DMZ.

Dorasan Station

The northernmost train station in South Korea, Dorasan Station was, at one point, a functioning train station. It opened on the Lunar New Year holiday of 2002, when it received the first train to cross the Imjingang River in 52 years. It soon after came to global attention with a visit by then South Korean and US Presidents Kim Dae-jung and George W. Bush. Its highpoint came on December 11, 2007, when the first freight train passed through Dorasan Station on its way to the Kaesong Industrial Complex in North Korea, the first such train to cross the DMZ since the Korean War. In December 2008, however, a worsening of relations between the two Koreas led to suspension of inter-Korean freight service.

The station is now closed to train traffic, but it is open for tourists. It's a beautiful, modern station with a number of unification-themed photos and works of art. It is hoped that it will one day be an important piece of the Iron Silk Road, a rail network that would link Korea and China to the European market.

CHEORWON

Up toward the DMZ, about two and a half hours from Seoul, is the small town of Cheorwon. At one time, it was a bustling transportation hub, the junction of the old colonial road and rail networks that linked Seoul with northern Korea and Manchuria. Situated in a broad valley, its fields have for ages produced some of Korea's finest rice.

In 1945, however, the newly liberated Korea was divided into two zones of occupation, and Cheorwon, located north of the 38th Parallel, came under Soviet and, ultimately, North Korean rule. During the Korean War, it became a key link in the so-called "Iron Triangle," a major staging ground for North Korean and Chinese offensives on Seoul. In the summer of 1951, American and South Korean forces launched the last major offensive of the war to capture the Iron Triangle, and the town—or what little was left of it—was brought under South Korean control.

Spring flowers bloom in front of the ruins of the Workers' Party of Korea Building in Cheorwon.

By war's end, the once prosperous town of Cheorwon was, quite literally, no more. All that remained were a couple of lonely ruins amidst an almost lunar landscape. After the war, a new town sprung up about 10 km away, but the ruins of the old town—much of it designated off-limits to civilians—remained preserved.

Today, the ruins of Cheorwon are a tourist destination, symbols of the tragedy of national division and the horrors of war. The town is also home to a monument to the Battle of White Horse Hill, one of the most ferocious battles of the war, and the Seungilgyo Bridge, which is often called Korea's "Bridge on the River Kwai."

Ruins of Workers' Party of Korea Building

The ruins of the old Cheorwon office of the Workers' Party of Korea, the ruling party of North Korea, is perhaps Korea's most haunting symbol of division and war.

One of only a few buildings in Cheorwon whose walls remained standing once the guns fell silent, the bombed-out skeleton, with its

Battle scars on the Workers' Party of Korea Building, Cheorwon.

bullet- and shell-scarred façade, recalls
images of post-war Germany. Around it is
nothing but fields and hills where a once-
prosperous downtown had been—a jarring
reminder of the complete devastation the
war visited upon the city.

The original building was constructed in
1946 by the North Koreans using Soviet
engineering techniques. The result was a
sturdy three-story concrete building of the
Soviet style frequently encountered in
North Korea and the former Eastern Bloc.
The office was erected, it is said, using forced labor and
contributions of rice squeezed from the locals.

As this was the headquarters of the local branch of the
communist Workers' Party of Korea, within its walls party leaders
kept an eye on the local population, planned espionage and
guerrilla activities against the South, and questioned and tortured
those accused of anti-communist activities. Bones, bullets, and
barbed wire were discovered in a tunnel behind the office.

Like the rest of Cheorwon, the old building suffered greatly in the
battles for the Iron Triangle in mid-1951. Repeated shelling left it a
burnt-out shell. The steps leading to its entrance bear the marks of
tank treads. It is all very surreal.

Today, the ruins are seen as a symbol of Korea's division and the
horror of fratricidal war. On occasion, the site is used for concerts
and performances.

Old Woljeong-ri Station and Cheorwon Peace Observatory

Located just in front of the southern side of the DMZ is a small
train station. Old Woljeong-ri Station—actually a 1988
restoration—is the closest train station to the DMZ in South Korea,

Bullet-riddled remains of a train behind the station. (left) Old Woljeong-ri Station. (right)

although trains stopped running this far north long ago. It is kept around for symbolic reasons. Behind the station are an old train platform, a rusting sign, and the twisted skeletal remains of a North Korean transport train bombed by the Americans during the war.

Nearby is an observatory for crane watching—cranes flourish in the tranquil, generally uninhabited DMZ—and the Cheorwon Peace Observatory. Recently built and equipped with a state-of-the-art monorail (tickets: 3,000 won), it offers a rare chance to look out into the DMZ and beyond into North Korea.

Battle of White Horse Hill Monument

About a ten-minute drive from the Workers' Party of Korea building is the Battle of White Horse Hill Monument. Located at the top of the hill for which the battle was named, it consists of both a memorial for the fallen and a monument celebrating the ROK 9th Division's victory in the bloodiest engagement in the Iron Triangle campaign. The complex is dominated by a 22.5 meter memorial tower you can see for miles around. There is also a museum with the personal effects of Gen. Kim Chong-oh, the commander of the ROK 9th Infantry Division who led the South Koreans to victory.

Seungilgyo Bridge

Several kilometers from the old Workers' Party of Korea building is a handsome—if somewhat aged—concrete arch bridge that spans a gorge of the Hantanggang River. It is a particularly beautiful spot any time of year, especially if you like old bridges.

According to popular belief, the Seungilgyo Bridge was started by the North Koreans in 1948 and completed by the South Koreans after the war. In you look closely, you will see that the north and south halves of the bridge—most notably the decorative arches—are clearly different. There has been some debate about the name; some claim it is taken from the names of the South and North Korean leaders at the time (Rhee Syngman—pronounced Lee Seung-man in Korean—and Kim Il-sung), while others claim it is named for Col. Park Seung-il, who was killed in action after leading his troops

Historic Seungilgyo Bridge (on right)

Old checkpoint in front of Seungilgyo Bridge.

across the Hantangang River. The original name of the bridge was the Hantangyo Bridge, after the river it spans.

Because of the tragic history of national division and war that the bridge architecturally represents, it is sometimes called Korea's "Bridge on the River Kwai."

While no one doubts the tragic romance of the bridge's history, it may not, in fact, be true. Recent research has turned up journal entries and photos that suggest that the bridge was begun by the colonial Japanese and completed by the US 79th Engineer Construction Battalion. This is the explanation given on the bridge's tourist information board.

• **Getting There:** Getting to the ruins of the Workers' Party of Korea building is easy enough. Take Seoul Subway Line 1 to Dongducheon Station. Transfer there to the Gyeongwon Line commuter train and get off at the last stop (and we do mean last—any further and you are in North Korea) at Sintan-ri. From in front of the station, catch a local bus that will drop you off at the ruins. In all, the trip will take approximately two hours from downtown Seoul.

To get to some of the other sites in Cheorwon, you're going to need your own transportation (or a taxi). Entry to sites in the Civilian Control Zone is permitted four times a day: 9:30, 10:30 am, 1, 2:30 pm (March to October), 9:30, 10:30 am, 1, 2 pm (November to February). Be sure to bring your passport. The Seungilgyo Bridge can also be reached via taxi. Call (033) 450-5558 for more information.

THE PUNCHBOWL—YANGGU

More precisely known as the Haean Basin, this bowl-shaped depression, surrounded by rugged hills, was called the "Punchbowl" by the Americans during the Korean War. The name stuck. The hills and peaks surrounding the Punchbowl were the scene of some of the bloodiest fighting of the Korean War. Today, the Punchbowl is home to a museum dedicated to the Punchbowl battles and the Ulji Observatory. Also near the Punchbowl is Mt. Daeam-san, which is home to Yongneup, a highland moor and one of Korea's protected wetlands.

• **Getting There:** Buses to Yanggu depart from Seoul's Dongseoul Terminal; the trip takes about two hours. From Yanggu Bus Terminal, take a local bus to Haean (in the Punchbowl). To visit the Ulji Observatory, visitors must apply for an entry license at the Yanggu Unification Hall (02-3480-2674) in Haean-myeon by 4pm on the day of their visit.

Fertile fields in the so-called "Punchbowl"

PEACE DAM — HWACHEON

The Peace Dam is one of those Cold War oddities you can find only in Korea. In 1986, the North Koreans began work on a large dam not far from the DMZ. South Korean officials feared the North Koreans might use the dam to flood the Bukhangang River, causing mass destruction and wiping out Seoul. To counter the North Koreans, South Korea began work in 1987 on its own dam to stop any potential North Korean "water attack," with ordinary South Koreans—including schoolchildren—donating money to the effort. The gargantuan dam is 601 meter long and 125 meter high; unlike

other dams, the Peace Dam has no reservoir—its one and only purpose is to stop any water surge caused by the North Koreans. The dam is located in a wild, rugged, and remote area of central Korea, connected to the outside world by a scenic road that takes you through the mountains and high passes. The dam has been rededicated as a peace park, dotted with massive 37.5 ton Korean Buddhist bells crafted from spent shell casings taken from about 30 war zones around the world, including some from the Korean War.

• **Getting There:** Buses to Hwacheon depart from Seoul's Dongseoul Terminal; the trip takes about two and a half hours. From Hwacheon, take a city bus to the Peace Dam (7:10, 12 pm, 5, 7 pm).

The Peace Dam. Built to prevent a North Korean "water attack," it has been rechristened as a monument of peace.

DMZ Observatories

A series of observatories are located along the length of the DMZ, allowing visitors a look into the no-man's-land and the forbidden North.

KEY OBSERVATORY

Like the Typhoon Observatory, this lookout point was named for the army unit that built it. It provides breathtaking views of the mountainous terrain.

TYPHOON OBSERVATORY

Named for the South Korean Army unit that built it, the Typhoon Observatory is the South Korean observatory closest to North Korea, located just 800 m from the MDL.

Gaeseong

Woljeong-ri Station

Cheor

1st Tunnel

Panmunjeom

Yeoncheon

Ganghwa Peace Observatory

3rd Tunnel

Imjingak

DORA OBSERVATORY

Located not far from the Third Tunnel of Aggression, this observatory, built upon a disused Army observation post, provides views of the North Korean city of Gaeseong and Mt. Songak-san.

Paju

ODUSAN UNIFICATION OBSERVATORY

Located a mere 40 minutes from Seoul, this observatory sits atop a hill overlooking the confluence of the Hangang and Imjingang rivers, with North Korea on the opposite shore. It provides rare views of North Korean civilians and soldiers.

Seoul

West Sea

A   B   C

1

2

3

4

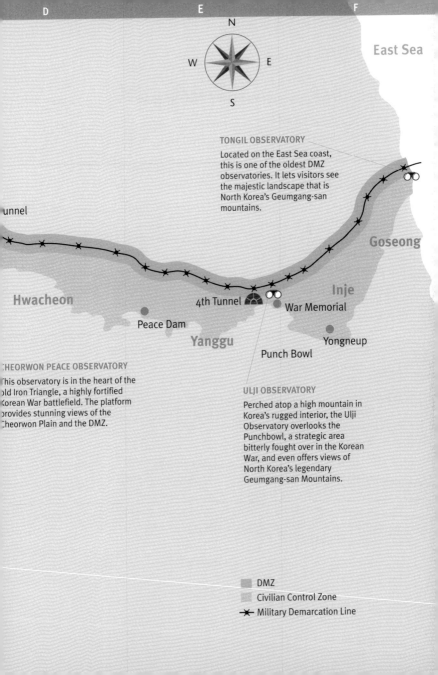

TONGIL OBSERVATORY

Located on the East Sea coast, this is one of the oldest DMZ observatories. It lets visitors see the majestic landscape that is North Korea's Geumgang-san mountains.

CHEORWON PEACE OBSERVATORY

This observatory is in the heart of the old Iron Triangle, a highly fortified Korean War battlefield. The platform provides stunning views of the Cheorwon Plain and the DMZ.

ULJI OBSERVATORY

Perched atop a high mountain in Korea's rugged interior, the Ulji Observatory overlooks the Punchbowl, a strategic area bitterly fought over in the Korean War, and even offers views of North Korea's legendary Geumgang-san Mountains.

East Sea

Goseong

Inje

Hwacheon

4th Tunnel

War Memorial

Peace Dam

Yanggu

Yongneup

Punch Bowl

unnel

- DMZ
- Civilian Control Zone
- Military Demarcation Line

THE DMZ AS A HISTORY MUSEUM

Visitors to the DMZ and its surrounding towns will find a wealth of historical sites including everything from evidence of Paleolithic culture to Joseon-era Buddhist relics.

Jeongok-ri Paleolithic Sites

Jeongok-ri is a small village in Yeoncheon County, a largely rural community that abuts the DMZ in northern Gyeonggi-do. A peaceful place not too different from other Korean farming towns, Jeongok-ri came to the world's attention in 1978 when Greg Bowen, a US soldier based at nearby Dongducheon, came across what he believed to be an important stone artifact while visiting a local resort. He brought the artifact to Kim Won-ryong, a professor at Seoul National University. Kim and another professor, Jung Young-hwa of Yeugnam University, determined the stone implement to be an Acheulean hand axe—a startling find, as this flew in the face of American archaeologist Hallam L. Movius' so-called "Movius Line," which posited that East Asian cultures never developed hand axes. Further discoveries at Jeongok-ri have prompted a reexamination of our understanding of the development of Paleolithic culture.

Over 4,000 Paleolithic artifacts have been discovered at the Jeongok-ri site, including hand axes, awls, and hammers. The artifacts are believed to date from 270,000 to 100,000 years ago. Also found were the bones of wild pigs and pollen, indicating that these early inhabitants had an understanding of the surrounding environment. The archeological site is now a park with exhibits and viewing facilities.

• **Getting There:** The Jeongok-ri Archeological Site is within walking distance of Jeongok Station on the Gyeongui Line. It's a lengthy walk, though, so you might wish to take a taxi from the station.

Dolmens

Dolmens are megalithic tombs, usually composed of three or four upright stones that hold up a large, horizontal capstone. They are a global historical and cultural development in the Neolithic Age following the appearance of funerary and ritual monuments. Korea has  the largest concentration of dolmens in the world, with most dating from the 1st millennium BC.

Ganghwa Island, located just south of the DMZ (parts of the island are, in fact, within the Civilian Control Line), is home to many of the early tombs. There are 157 dolmens spread out across the island, but they are particularly concentrated north of Mt. Goryeo-san. The most impressive of Ganghwa's dolmens is the Jiseongmyo, Korea's largest dolmen, with a capstone weighing over 80 tons. It is considered a "Northern-type" dolmen, with relatively high supporting stones. "Southern-type" dolmens, which make up the bulk of Korea's dolmens, feature shorter supporting stones. Interestingly, dolmens of both the Northern and Southern type can be found along the DMZ, indicating that the line may have marked a cultural dividing line many, many years ago.

Thanks to their historical and cultural significance, Korea's dolmens have been registered as a UNESCO World Heritage Site.

• **Getting There:** Take a bus from Seoul's Sinchon Bus Terminal to Ganghwa Bus Terminal. From there, take a local bus to Bugeun-ri.

Dopiansa Temple

Dopiansa Temple in Cheorwon, Gangwon-do is not one of Korea's largest temples, and certainly not one of its best known. In fact, for decades, it was off-limits to most civilians, located well beyond the Civilian Control Line. Since the readjustment of the Civilian Control Line, however, it is now located outside the line and can be freely visited by tourists.

The temple was founded in 865 by Doseon Guksa, one of the greatest Buddhist monks of his day. The temple is best known for its Vairocana Buddha, a seated Buddha that was made of iron, crafted in the year of the temple's founding. In fact, it is thanks to this statue that the temple was founded. According to one historical record, the Buddha was being sent to another temple, but it was lost during the delivery. Soon, it was found in its current location, and Doseon Guksa had a temple built. The Buddha has been designated National Treasure No. 63.

Dopiansa has a three-story stone pagoda that also dates from the founding of the temple and has been designated Treasure No. 223.

• **Getting There:** Take a bus to Dopiansa from Dongsong in Cheorwon. Buses to Dongsong depart from Seoul's Suyu-ri.

Castle of Gungye

Within the DMZ itself, in the town of Cheorwon, is the old capital of the kingdom of Taebong (901-918), a regional upstart that would become Goryeo, the dynasty that would rule a united Korea from 918 to 1392.

Taebong was founded by the charismatic leader Gungye, a brilliant if tyrannical one-eyed ex-Buddhist monk. Rebelling against the kingdom of Silla, Korea's then ruling dynasty, he proclaimed the kingdom of Taebong—also called Later Goguryeo, in reference to the ancient kingdom of Goguryeo (37 BC-AD 668)—in 901, with himself as king. The kingdom consisted of much of central Korea, including areas around the DMZ. He placed his capital in Cheorwon, a mountainous region that was easily defensible (in the Korean War, this same region would earn the name "the Iron Triangle").

As a former Buddhist monk, Gungye actively promoted the religion of Buddhism and incorporated Buddhist ceremonies into the new kingdom. Even after Gungye was dethroned by his own generals and replaced by Wang Geon, the man who would rule over a united Korea as the first king of Goryeo, this Buddhist influence would continue, playing a major role in shaping the culture of medieval Korea.

As the ruins of Gungye's capital lie in the DMZ itself, visitors cannot see it. Moreover, excavation work and research have been hampered by political realities. In the future, inter-Korean peace may allow for proper archeological studies to be conducted on the castle site and other historical sites within and underneath the DMZ.

APPENDIX

OTHER INFORMATION

Tours of the DMZ

Tense the relations between the two Koreas might be, but the DMZ—and the JSA in particular—is one of the country's top tourist attractions. Visits to the JSA require a guided tour (several companies offer this), but visits to other parts of the DMZ can be undertaken by individual travelers. Keep in mind, however, that the DMZ and Civilian Control Zone can be placed off-limits depending on the security situation.

USO TOURS OF THE JSA

The most popular tour to the DMZ is the JSA tour offered by the USO, which provides leisure and recreational opportunities to US military personnel. The tour is open to civilians, too. In addition to the JSA, these tours also visit the Third Tunnel of Aggression and Dora Observatory. At US$70 for civilians, these tours are quite cheap compared to other tours to the DMZ.

More Info: (02) 795-3028, http://affiliates.uso.org/korea/

TOURDMZ

This company offers a number of different tour packages, including tours to the JSA and the DMZ Barricades.

More Info: (02) 755-0073, www.tourdmz.com/english/main.php

PANMUNJOM TRAVEL CENTER

This is a private company that conducts tours to Panmunjeom between Tuesday and Friday. It also conducts combined tours of other areas of the DMZ, as well as tours with North Korean defectors.

More Info: (02) 771-5593~5, www.koreadmztour.com

DMZTOURKOREA.COM

The company runs tours of Panmunjeom, the DMZ tunnels, and even the iron fence of the DMZ.

More Info: (02) 706-4851, www.dmztourkorea.com

HIKING THE DMZ

The Korea Tourism Organization (KTO) is promoting tourism in the area along the DMZ and surrounding areas, which it has dubbed the Peace and Life Zone (PLZ). You can hike or drive the 545 km course, which encompasses history, culture, and ecological splendor. This is no organized tour—you do it yourself, although the KTO has a good guide to the course on its website (english.visitkorea.or.kr).

MORE ABOUT THE KOREAN WAR

Despite its status in the West as the "Forgotten War," the Korean War has been the subject of a number of excellent books, films, and online resources that provide a wealth of information on the conflict.

BOOKS

• Appleman, Roy E. *South to the Naktong, North to the Yalu* (June-November 1950). Washington, DC: United States Dept. of Defense, 1998.

• Mossman, Billy C. *Ebb and Flow* (November 1950-July 1951). Washington, DC: United States Army, 1990.

• Hermes, Walter G. *Truce Tent and Fighting Front* (the last two years). Washington, DC: United States Army, 1990.

These are the official US military histories of the Korean War. All three have very thorough accounts of the battles and negotiations of the Korean War, from the opening shots to the final armistice. Not much in the way of photos, but plenty of useful battle maps. Online versions available, too, at the website of the US Army Center of Military History (www.history.army.mil)

• Hastings, Max. *The Korean War*. New York: Simon & Schuster, 1988.

This wonderful work on the Korean War by a respected British war historian features rare interviews with Chinese and North Korean veterans, lending more insight into the war.

• Fehrenbach, T.R. *This Kind of War: The Classic Korean War History*. New York: Potomac Books Inc., 2001.

A frank look at the Korean War, told from both the broad perspective and that of the man in the trench. Considered a classic.

• Halberstam, David. *The Coldest Winter*. New York: Hyperion, 2007.

The last book by esteemed American journalist and historian David Halberstam, this work provides a very vivid account of the Korean War, contrasting the trials of the men at the front with the disastrous mistakes made by their commanders.

• Rich, John. *Korean War in Color: A Correspondent's Retrospective on a Forgotten War*. Seoul: Seoul Selection, 2010.

Veteran war reporter John Rich's color photographs of the Korean War bring the conflict home, making history feel contemporary. The first of its kind, the book contains images of both soldiers and civilians, allowing the reading to better understand the impact of the fighting.

• Salmon, Andrew. *To the Last Round: The Epic British Stand on the Imjin River, Korea 1951*. London: Aurum Press, 2009.

This riveting Korean War account focuses on one of the war's most important—yet largely unknown—battles, the epic struggle of Britain's 29th Infantry Brigade in the Battle of Imjin River. The many exclusive interviews with veterans lend great insight into the effects the war had on the individual soldier.

ONLINE RESOURCES

• **Korean War Project** www.koreanwar.org
With a special focus on veteran and KIA/MIA information, the website is a trove of information about the Korean War.

• **The Korean War** http://www.rt66.com/~korteng/
Maintained by US Navy and Korean War veteran Bert Kortegaard, this site has a ton of information and photos from the war, including documentary texts.

MOVIES

• *JSA (2000)*
This blockbuster by director Park Chan-wook, starring top Korean actors Lee Young-ae, Lee Byung-hun, and Song Kang-ho, weaves a tragic tale of friendship between North and South Korean soldiers at the DMZ. It was a hit with audiences, setting box office records, and was even praised by American director Quentin Tarantino, who called it one of his favorite films since 1992.

• *Tae Guk Gi: The Brotherhood of War* (2004)
Often compared to *Saving Private Ryan*, this 2004 Korean blockbuster tells the tale of two South Korean brothers fighting in the Korean War. Spectacular yet brutal, the film captures the horror of the conflict with unflinching depictions of battles, massacres, and social strife unleashed by the conflict.

• *Welcome to Dongmakgol* (2005)
Set in an idyllic mountain village in the Korean War, this Korean film tries to transcend war as the villagers bring together North Koreans, South Koreans, and Americans in a tale that mixes fantasy, comedy, and tragedy.

• *The Bridges at Toko-Ri* (1954)
Unlike World War II and Vietnam, the Korean War has gotten scant attention from Hollywood. This film, based on a novel by the same name by James A. Michener, is considered one of the best and depicts the campaign by US Navy pilots to take out heavily defended bridges in North Korea.

• *Korean War in Color* (2007)
This US-made documentary provides rarely seen color footage to introduce the Korean War from start to finish. Includes footage from the Incheon Landing, the Battle of Nakdong Perimeter, and the Battle of Chosin Reservoir.

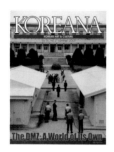

The content of this book is based on articles published in *Koreana* Vol. 15, No. 2, Summer 2001. Chapter 1, 2, 3, and 5 were newly written by Robert Koehler, and Chapter 4 is an edited version of Ham Kwang-bok's article "The Demilitarized Zone: Home to Nature Evolving in an Unforeseen Direction."

CONTRIBUTORS

Robert Koehler, Ham Kwang-bok

PHOTOGRAPHS

US Army photo
By Edward N. Johnson 5, 7, 13, 15, 18, 19, 53, 54, 55, 57, 59, 63, 64, 66, 68, 71, 72, 80
By TSgt(s) Renee' Sitler 21
US Department of Defense 17, 32, 33, 48, 49
By F. Kazukaitis 12
By Capt. F. L. Scheiber 40
By SSgt. Aaron D. Allmon II 42

(* Presence of U.S. Government media does not imply endorsement.)

Robert Koehler 21, 25, 37, 38, 50, 75, 76, 77, 78, 81, 82, 83, 84, 85, 86, 88
Yonhap Photo 8, 11, 14, 20, 21, 23, 28, 30, 41, 45, 87, 94
Image Today 60, 61, 70
Ryu Seung-hoo 40, 93
Lee Jin-hyuk 76, 96
John Rich 47

Credits

Publisher	Kim Hyung-geun
Editor	Lee Jin-hyuk
Copy Editor	Colin A. Mouat
Proof Reader	Chung Kyung-a
Designer	Min So-young

DEATH COMES TO
ROCK SPRINGS

Jarrod Kilkline is in trouble with the army, the law, and a persistent bounty hunter. Fleeing from capture, he heads into the Rocky Mountains where he rescues Brian Tyler, who has been left for dead by the three Jackson brothers. Tyler is a preacher on his way to the town of Rock Springs, and Jarrod reluctantly agrees to accompany him. But when the Jacksons reappear on the scene, will Jarrod side with them or with the law in the final showdown?